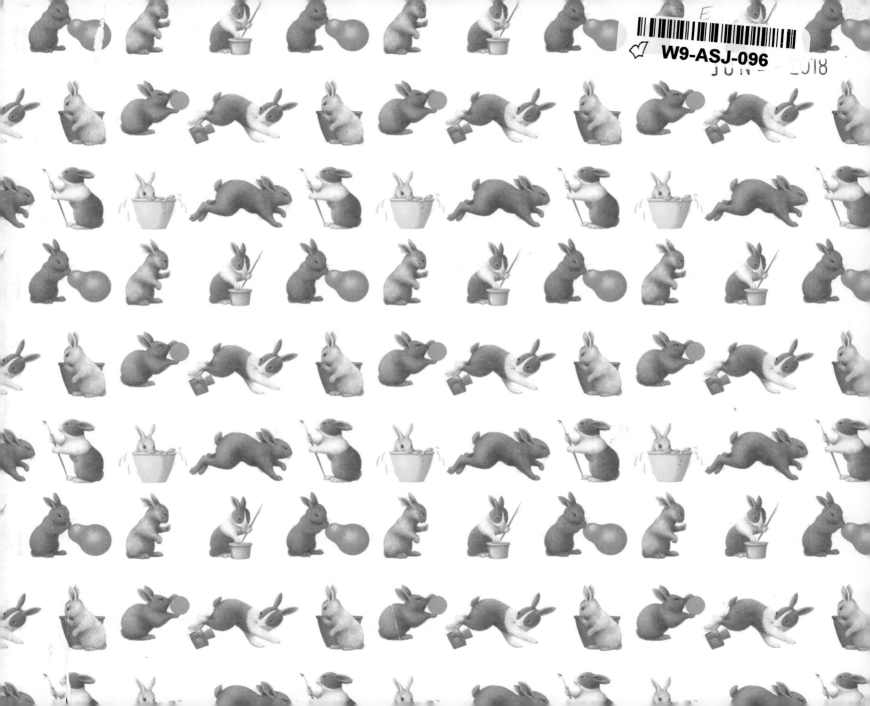

WHITE RABBIT'S
COLORS

LITTLE RABBITS

ALAN BAKER

KINGFISHER
NEW YORK

KINGFISHER
LONDON & NEW YORK

First published 1994 by Kingfisher
This edition published 2017 by Kingfisher
Published in the United States by Kingfisher,
175 Fifth Ave., New York, NY 10010
Kingfisher is an imprint of Macmillan Children's Books, London.
All rights reserved.

Copyright © Alan Baker 1994

Distributed in the U.S. and Canada by Macmillan,
175 Fifth Ave., New York, NY 10010

Library of Congress Cataloging-in-Publication data
has been applied for.

ISBN: 978-0-7534-7320-7 (HB)
ISBN: 978-0-7534-7321-4 (PB)

Kingfisher books are available for special promotions
and premiums. For details contact: Special Markets
Department, Macmillan, 175 Fifth Ave.,
New York, NY 10010.

For more information, please visit
www.kingfisherbooks.com

Printed in China
9 8 7 6 5 4 3 2 1
1TR/1116/WKT/UG/157MA

One day, White Rabbit found
three big tubs of paint,
red, yellow, and blue.

Sunshine yellow,
she thought.
Lovely.

A quick dip
and ...

... yellow rabbit,
bright as the Sun.

Now what about red, thought Rabbit.

What's this?
Orange Rabbit?
Look. Red and yellow
together make
orange!

Time for
a wash,
thought
Rabbit.

Red on its own this time.

Splash!

Red Rabbit,
sizzling hot red.

How cool blue looks, thought Rabbit.

What's this? Purple Rabbit?
Look. Red and blue
together make purple.
I'm a very important
Royal Purple
Rabbit.

Princess
Purple
Rabbit
in the shower.

Blue will do,
thought Rabbit.

Blue Rabbit,
icy cold blue.
Brrr.

How warm
yellow looks,
thought Rabbit.

What's this?
Green Rabbit.
Look. Blue
and yellow
together make
green!

Hooray! Brown Rabbit. Lovely warm brown.
Blue, yellow, and red together make brown.
And brown's just right for me.

Now what would happen? thought Rabbit.

All that's left is
a little red paint.

Oh dear,
no more
water.